QUICK PRACTICE
WRITING SKILLS
Grades 2-3

Dozens of Reproducible Pages
That Give Kids Practice
in Grammar, Mechanics, Spelling,
and Other Key Writing Skills

by Marcia Miller and Martin Lee

NEW YORK • TORONTO • LONDON • AUKLAND • SYDNEY
MEXICO CITY • NEW DELHI • HONG KONG • BUENOS AIRES

SCHOLASTIC
Teaching
Resources

Cover design by Maria Lilja
Cover illustration by Mike Gordon
Interior design by Jeffrey Dorman
Interior illustrations by Maxie Chambliss

ISBN 0-439-37075-2
Copyright © 2003 by Marcia Miller and Martin Lee
All rights reserved.
Printed in the U.S.A.

1 2 3 4 5 6 7 8 9 10   40   09 08 07 06 05 04 03

CONTENTS

Part 1:
General Concepts of Writing

Part 2:
Conventions of Grammar, Mechanics, and Style

Part 3:
Steps of the Writing Process

Part 4:
Researching and Gathering Information

ABOUT THIS BOOK

As teachers, we want to guide students to become good writers, to empower them to communicate in writing as freely, naturally, and effectively as they do when speaking.

> **Quick Practice Writing Skills: Grades 2–3** is one of a series of four grade-specific books for students K–8. Each book has a dual purpose—to sharpen students' skills as writers, and to provide ways you can help to prepare them for success when they take standardized tests of writing.

Because writing is such a crucial measure of one's ability to communicate, many school districts and state departments of education utilize approved lists of writing standards at each grade level that students are expected to meet. Writing has increasingly become a regular component of standardized testing. In addition to short-answer items, standardized tests ask students to plan, write, edit, and present a finished piece of independent writing on a given topic.

> **Quick Practice Writing Skills: Grades 2–3** gives students opportunities to practice and develop some of the key skills and strategies of the writing process. By using this book, your students will grow as writers.

Good writing doesn't happen by chance. We become skilled writers because we write—and keep on writing. We write to express fact, opinion, humor, memory, feelings, admiration, criticism, and creativity. We write to instruct, inform, and interpret. The more we write, the more we understand about writing. We learn to mold a piece of writing to a given purpose, to fit a particular audience, and to achieve a certain result.

> **Quick Practice Writing Skills: Grades 2–3** addresses the many ways that standardized tests may evaluate students' ability to express themselves as writers.

The activity pages you will find in *Quick Practice Writing Skills: Grades 2–3* are based on recent versions of an assortment of testing instruments, as well as a compilation of standards applied to language arts and writing. They provide various formats and levels of complexity within the targeted grade range. Each page or activity is self-contained and concise enough to be used as a warm-up or follow-up to a related lesson within your writing curriculum. While some activity pages have questions with only one correct answer, others are open-ended, mirroring many of the newer standardized tests.

In developing these books, we have drawn upon a wide range of materials and resources. One very useful Web site you may wish to explore can be found at **www.mcrel.org**. Here, you can examine a wealth of materials about standards-based education in general as well as specific curriculum standards, testing, and position papers.

> **Quick Practice Writing Skills: Grades 2–3** can help your students develop greater confidence and feel more relaxed in a test-taking situation.

Test taking is like any task—the more it is practiced, the less daunting it becomes. The activities in this book cannot substitute for the standardized testing instruments your students will take, as mandated by your school district and/or state education department. But they can decrease some of the anxiety and mystery surrounding standards and standardized testing.

USING THIS BOOK

Quick Practice Writing Skills: Grades 2–3 has been organized into four main sections that reflect the general aspects of writing:

1. General Concepts of Writing

2. Conventions of Grammar, Mechanics, and Style

3. Steps of the Writing Process

4. Researching and Gathering Information

Within each section, we address a particular aspect of writing in quantifiable and grade-appropriate ways. Obviously, in a book of this length, it is not possible to test everything, nor can one book be certain to dovetail with every aspect of your particular writing curriculum or the standards your students are expected to meet. Simply regard the sections as broad-stroke plans of organization.

Standardized writing tests include short-answer and free-form writing tasks. In this book we include both. You will find certain writing skills exercised in short-answer items. You will also find ample opportunities for open-ended writing.

At the back of the book, you will find suggested ideas for writing group stories; a reproducible "bubble sheet," which gives children practice using a common standardized test format; and a Writer's Self-Evaluation Checklist children can use as an aid to refine their writing before handing it in. You will also find selected answers and brief teacher notes.

Here are some suggestions for using *Quick Practice Writing Skills: Grades 2-3:*

- Present the activity pages in any order you wish.

- Allow pages to be completed independently, in pairs, in small groups, or by the whole class as a group activity. Use your best judgment.

- You may have to read directions aloud to remove a potential stumbling block for less-independent readers.

- You may wish to do a sample exercise together, as you see fit.

- Feel free to take any format we provide in this book and revise it to fit your students' needs. Use any exercise as a springboard for similar activities you create, or extend and develop it into a complete lesson or project.

- Take the time to review and discuss students' responses. Analyze the responses for diagnostic use.

- Print and distribute (or post) the Tried & True Test-Taking Tips on page 6. Discuss them with your class and invite students to add their own useful suggestions to the list.

- You might introduce RUSTY, the test-taking mascot. Use a stuffed animal or hand puppet as a friendly device to reinforce five simple steps for good test taking:

[R]ead the directions.

[U]nderstand what to do.

[S]earch for clues.

[T]hink about your answer.

[Y]ou can do it!

TRIED & TRUE TEST-TAKING TIPS

- Get plenty of rest the night before the test.
- Eat a healthy breakfast.
- Wear comfortable clothing.
- Get to school on time!
- Gather all the materials you need—sharp pencils, erasers, scratch paper, and so on.
- Bring your positive attitude!
- Listen to or read instructions carefully.
- If you don't understand something, raise your hand and ask for help.
- Work purposefully and carefully.
- Read the whole question and all the given answer choices before marking anything.
- Don't let other people distract you. Stick to the task.
- Try to answer ALL questions. But if you are stumped, take a deep breath and move on. Come back to the question later.
- If you change your mind, erase your first answer completely.
- If you aren't sure, choose the answer that seems best to you.
- Double-check your answers, if you have time.
- Proofread your writing.
- Neatness counts! Make sure that all your writing is legible.

Name ....

TEST-TAKING PRACTICE

Follow the directions.

1. Draw a circle around the clock.

2. Circle the letter.   **6**   **#**   **?**   **h**

3. Underline the basket.

4. Connect the 8's.

5. Mark the middle oval.

6. Fill in the blank.   **30, 40, ____, 60, 70, 80**

7. Match the people and hats.

8. Draw an X on the one that does NOT belong.

MORE TEST-TAKING PRACTICE

Follow the directions.

1. Mark the zebra.

5. Underline the clown.

2. Which is the fork?

6. Draw an X on the unhappy child.

3. Shade the space for lipstick.

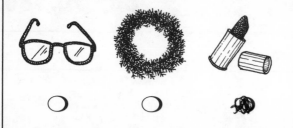

7. Circle the letter R.

D P R F

4. Fill the space for the fruit.

8. Match the pictures.

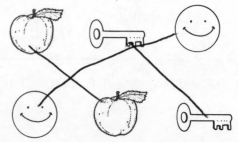

PART 1:

GENERAL CONCEPTS OF WRITING

PLAN A TRIP

Let's go camping in the woods!   Draw three things to bring.
Write about what you draw.

Fla _____

_____

_____

_____

_____

_____

_____

_____

_____

_____

_____

_____

Name ....

MAKE A LIST

What is in the science room?
Make a list. Draw pictures, too.

_____

_____

_____

_____

_____

_____

_____

_____

INVITE A FRIEND

Invite a friend to sleep over at your house.
Draw or write what to say.

_____

_____

_____

_____

Name ....

LEAVE A NOTE

Dad will be home soon.
Leave Dad a note.
Tell him where you have gone.
Don't forget to tell him why.

Name ....

MAKE A CHART

Look at the picture. Fill in the chart about who you see.

I SEE...	HOW MANY?

FINISH THE CHART

What do kids like to play with?
Write the words. Draw the pictures.

THINGS TO PLAY WITH

WORDS	PICTURES
_____	
_____	
_____	
_____	
_____	
_____	
_____	
_____	
_____	
_____	

LABELS (1)

Label each picture. Write a word on the line.

1.

2.

3.

4.

5.

6.

Name ....

LABELS (2)

Label each picture. Write a word on the line.

1.

2.

3.

4.

5.

6.

WRITE A WORD

Write a word that begins with the same sound the picture does.

1. _____

2. _____

3. _____

4. _____

5. _____

6. _____

7. _____

8.  _____

9. _____

10. _____

WORDS AND SPACES

Write a sentence about each picture.
Be sure to leave space between each word.

1.

_____

_____

_____

2.

_____

_____

_____

3.

_____

_____

_____

4.

_____

_____

_____

5.

_____

_____

_____

Name ....

TELL ABOUT IT (1)

Look at the picture. What is going on? Write about it.

_____

_____

_____

_____

_____

_____

_____

Name ....

TELL ABOUT IT (2)

Look at the picture. What is going on? Write about it.

_____

_____

_____

_____

_____

_____

MAKE A SENTENCE

Use all the words in each box to write a sentence.

1.
| old |
| the |
| is |
| cat |

_____

_____

_____

2.
| my |
| where |
| are |
| slippers |

_____

_____

_____

3.
| bake |
| some |
| cookies |
| let's |

_____

_____

_____

4.
| is |
| book |
| this |
| hard |
| too |

_____

_____

_____

5.
| right |
| who |
| answer |
| the |
| knows |

_____

_____

_____

WRITE SOME MORE

Finish the sentence. Then write another sentence that comes next.

1. That pizza was way too _____

_____

_____

2. I forgot to tell _____

_____

_____

3. Can you help us to _____

_____

_____

4. The music makes me want to _____

_____

_____

5. Dark clouds may mean that _____

_____

_____

Name ....

NAME THE GROUP (1)

Look at the group in each box. Circle the word that **names** it.
Then write a sentence about the group.

|  | birds
letters
feathers |

1. _____

_____

_____

| 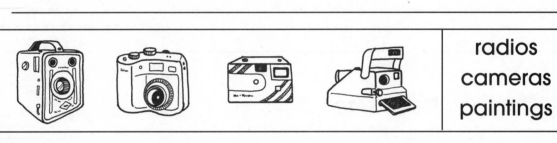 | radios
cameras
paintings |

2. _____

_____

_____

|  | boats
planes
trains |

3. _____

_____

_____

Name ....

NAME THE GROUP (2)

Look at the group in each box. Circle the word that names it.
Then write a sentence about the group.

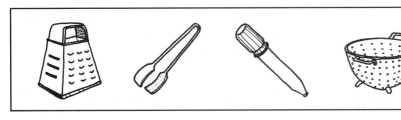

dental tools
garden tools
kitchen tools

1. _____

_____

_____

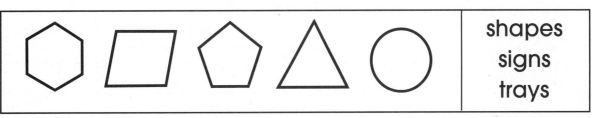

shapes
signs
trays

2. _____

_____

_____

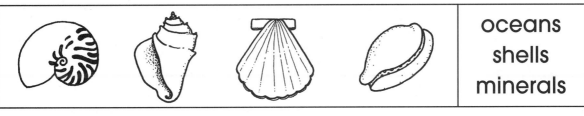

oceans
shells
minerals

3. _____

_____

_____

FINISH THE PARAGRAPHS

These paragraphs are not finished. Read
what is already written. Then add to it.

1. We went on a whale watch.
We left the dock at 7:30 in the
morning. It was a cloudy day. The wooden boat was old
but sturdy. There were about twenty _____

_____

_____

_____

_____

2. On the way back to shore, we were tired and hungry.
It had been a long day, but we had seen some great sights.
The whales seemed curious. They swam close to _____

_____

_____

_____

_____

Name ....

PUT IN ORDER (1)

Look at the pictures.

Which comes first? Write **1**.

Which comes next? Write **2**.

Which comes last? Write **3**.

Then write the story the pictures show.

_____

_____

_____

_____

_____

_____

PUT IN ORDER (2)

Look at the pictures.

Which comes first? Write **1**.

Which comes next? Write **2**.

Which comes after that? Write **3**.

Which comes last? Write **4**.

Then write the story the pictures show.

_____

_____

_____

_____

_____

_____

_____

Name ....

WHAT HAPPENED <u>BEFORE</u>?

Look at the big picture.

Which small picture came *before*?

Check ✔ that picture. Tell how you know.

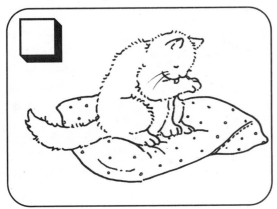

_____

_____

_____

_____

_____

Name ....

WHAT HAPPENS **NEXT?**

Look at the big picture.
Which small picture comes *next*?
Check ✔ that picture. Tell how you know.

_____

_____

_____

_____

_____

Name ....

TELL A STORY (1)

Look at the pictures. Write the story they show.

_____

_____

_____

_____

_____

_____

_____

_____

Name ....

TELL A STORY (2)

Look at the pictures. Write the story they show.

_____

_____

_____

_____

_____

_____

_____

_____

WRITE A REPORT

**Look at the picture. What do you think is going on?
Write a report that gives your idea.**

Name ....

TAKE A MESSAGE

Your teacher calls your house. She wants to talk to your mom.
But your mom is not home. Fill out the form to leave a phone
message. (You can make up the information.)

Message for: _____

Date: _____ Time of Call: _____

Name of Caller: _____

Who is this person? _____

Message: _____

_____

_____

_____

_____

Caller's Phone Number: _____

Who took this message? _____

PART 2:

CONVENTIONS OF GRAMMAR, MECHANICS, AND STYLE

FIND THE NOUN

Mark the letter of the word that is a noun.

1. That purple coat has shiny buttons.
$\quad$ Ⓐ $\quad$ Ⓑ $\quad$ Ⓒ $\quad$ Ⓓ

2. Why do clouds get so puffy?
$\quad$ Ⓐ $\quad$ Ⓑ $\quad$ Ⓒ $\quad$ Ⓓ

3. Actually, my best friend is younger than I am.
$\quad$ Ⓐ $\quad$ Ⓑ $\quad$ Ⓒ $\quad$ Ⓓ

4. All kids bring their lunches to school on Field Day.
$\quad$ Ⓐ $\quad$ Ⓑ $\quad$ Ⓒ $\quad$ Ⓓ

5. She bought a colorful postcard of Maine.
$\quad$ Ⓐ $\quad$ Ⓑ $\quad$ Ⓒ $\quad$ Ⓓ

6. Henry is the fastest runner in our class.
$\quad$ Ⓐ $\quad$ Ⓑ $\quad$ Ⓒ $\quad$ Ⓓ

7. Do you know where we can find blue polish?
$\quad$ Ⓐ $\quad$ Ⓑ $\quad$ Ⓒ $\quad$ Ⓓ

8. Long ago, pencils did not have erasers on them.
$\quad$ Ⓐ $\quad$ Ⓑ $\quad$ Ⓒ $\quad$ Ⓓ

9. If you ask me, that movie was boring.
$\quad$ Ⓐ $\quad$ Ⓑ $\quad$ Ⓒ $\quad$ Ⓓ

10. Neither of us has read that booklet.
$\quad$ Ⓐ $\quad$ Ⓑ $\quad$ Ⓒ $\quad$ Ⓓ

11. With this song, we pray for peace on earth.
$\quad$ Ⓐ $\quad$ Ⓑ $\quad$ Ⓒ $\quad$ Ⓓ

12. That lamp is the brightest one in the whole house.
$\quad$ Ⓐ $\quad$ Ⓑ $\quad$ Ⓒ $\quad$ Ⓓ

Name ....

NOUN NAMES

Each sentence has a noun shown in **boldface**. Write whether that noun names a *person*, a *place*, a *thing*, or an *idea*.

1. The giant **panda** is a kind of bear. _____

2. Pandas live in the forests of **China**. _____

3. **Scientists** thought they were related to raccoons.

_____

4. Pandas can't roar, but they make a bleating **sound**.

_____

5. Have you read *Giant Panda* by **Melissa** Kim?

_____

6. Pandas are popular with **visitors** to the zoo.

_____

7. The zoo shop sells a cute panda **puppet**.

_____

8. Zoo pandas don't have **freedom** to roam.

_____

9. Pandas cannot walk on their hind **legs**.

_____

10. Pandas spend most of their **time** eating.

_____

11. Ruth **Harkness** brought the first live giant panda from China to America in 1936.

_____

12. Capturing pandas is now against the **law** in China.

_____

WRITE THE PLURAL

Fill in the chart of nouns. The first one has been done for you.

	ONE...	MANY...
1.	tiger	tigers
2.	soldier	
3.	desk	
4.	bench	
5.	fox	
6.	city	
7.	family	
8.	turkey	
9.	leaf	
10.	life	
11.	child	
12.	man	
13.	foot	
14.	goose	
15.	deer	

WRITE THE SINGULAR

Fill in the chart of nouns. The first one has been done for you.

	LOTS OF...	BUT ONLY ONE...
1.	faces	face
2.	apples	
3.	chairs	
4.	lunches	
5.	boxes	
6.	candies	
7.	berries	
8.	monkeys	
9.	knives	
10.	halves	
11.	heroes	
12.	echoes	
13.	sheep	
14.	women	
15.	mice	

PICK THE PRONOUN

Circle the letter beside the pronoun that best completes the sentence.

1. Dad didn't bother to hang up _____ jacket.
   a. he   **b.** him   **c.** his   **d.** her

2. _____ just tossed the jacket onto the couch.
   a. He   **b.** Him   **c.** His   **d.** They

3. Queenie, our dog, needed a place to hide _____ bone.
   a. she   **b.** him   **c.** your   **d.** her

4. So _____ pushed it into the sleeve of the jacket.
   a. she   **b.** him   **c.** your   **d.** her

5. Dad remembered that _____ left a note in the jacket pocket.
   a. she   **b.** me   **c.** he   **d.** them

6. "Relax, dear. I'll get it for _____," said Mom.
   a. your   **b.** you   **c.** I   **d.** he

7. When she picked up the jacket, _____ felt too heavy.
   a. they   **b.** it   **c.** he   **d.** you

8. Something went *thud*, and Queenie ran in to see _____.
   a. him   **b.** them   **c.** it   **d.** I

9. "Well, Queenie," scolded Mom, "_____ are a rascal!"
   a. he   **b.** they   **c.** it   **d.** you

10. After that, _____ all had a good laugh together.
   a. we   **b.** us   **c.** them   **d.** my

Name ....

FIND THE VERB

Mark the letter of the word that is a verb.

1. <u>Many</u> <u>kinds</u> of animals <u>live</u> in
     (A)   (B)   (C)

    the <u>rain forest</u>.
          (D)

2. <u>Some</u> people <u>use</u> the word
     (A)   (B)

    jungle <u>instead</u> of rain forest.
    (C)   (D)

3. <u>Colorful</u> birds, such as <u>parrots</u>, <u>fly</u>
     (A)   (B)   (C)

    through the <u>treetops</u>.
             (D)

4. <u>Howler</u> <u>monkeys</u> <u>screech</u> at each <u>other</u> as they climb.
     (A)   (B)   (C)   (D)

5. Snakes <u>wind</u> around <u>branches</u> <u>and</u> slither on the <u>ground</u>.
        (A)   (B)   (C)   (D)

6. <u>You</u> can <u>hear</u> the <u>steady</u> hum of <u>insects</u> at work.
     (A)   (B)   (C)   (D)

7. Millions of creatures <u>make</u> <u>their</u> <u>homes</u> <u>in</u> rain forests.
                  (A)   (B)   (C) (D)

8. <u>One</u> rain-forest <u>butterfly</u> <u>has</u> wings <u>that</u> are a foot wide!
     (A)   (B)   (C)   (D)

9. Many <u>kinds</u> of plants <u>grow</u> <u>only</u> in <u>rain forests</u>.
        (A)   (B) (C)   (D)

10. <u>Scientists</u> <u>know</u> <u>of</u> <u>thousands</u> of kinds of ferns!
      (A)   (B) (C)   (D)

11. <u>But</u> don't forget: <u>People</u> <u>need</u> rain forests, <u>too</u>.
      (A)   (B)   (C)   (D)

12. They <u>eat</u> tropical <u>fruits</u>, <u>such</u> as mangoes and <u>pineapples</u>.
      (A)   (B)   (C)   (D)

PICK THE VERB FORM

Circle the letter beside the verb form that best completes the sentence.

1. Joe and I decided to _____ the swimming team.
   a. join   **b.** joining   **c.** joins

2. We _____ swim classes three times a week.
   a. takes   **b.** take   **c.** taking

3. Our swim coach _____ a medal in the Olympics.
   a. winned   **b.** won   **c.** win

4. She _____ us practice over and over.
   a. makes   **b.** make   **c.** maked

5. Last week, we _____ the butterfly stroke.
   a. learn   **b.** learned   **c.** learns

6. I think it _____ the hardest stroke to do.
   a. be   **b.** is   **c.** are

7. But I love to make the water _____ as I go.
   a. splash   **b.** splashes   **c.** splashed

8. Last time, I _____ too much water in my nose.
   a. get   **b.** gets   **c.** got

9. It _____ me cough and sneeze, but I got over it.
   a. make   **b.** made   **c.** making

10. Can you _____ to our swim meet next week?
   a. coming   **b.** came   **c.** come

USE THE VERB

Write a sentence using the verb given.

1. wrapped

_____

_____

2. sang

_____

_____

3. likes

_____

_____

4. wrote

_____

_____

5. were

_____

_____

6. will bring

_____

_____

Name ....

USE VERB TENSES

Write a form of the verb shown in **boldface** to finish each sentence. The first one has been done for you.

1. Yesterday I **ate** tuna for lunch, but today I will __eat__ pizza.

2. At her party last year, Jenny **blew** out only three candles. This year, she will _____ out all of them!

3. Today Jed **drinks** lemonade with his lunch, but yesterday he _____ milk.

4. Can you **dig** a hole as deep as the one we _____ over there?

5. Paco **brings** the snack for today because Ramon _____ the snack last time.

6. Ed **forgot** the words to the song, but I won't _____ them.

7. Lori **left** at five, but we won't _____ until seven.

8. We **saw** a great movie about frogs. Have you _____ it yet?

9. I'll **tell** you the silly joke that my cousin _____ me.

10. Can you **write** another poem as fine as the one you _____ about the sunset?

USE A BETTER VERB

These sentences have plain verbs. Rewrite each sentence using a more exciting verb.

1. Kevin <u>walked</u> to the ball field.

_____

2. The very hungry dog <u>ate</u> his supper.

_____

3. Marla <u>ran</u> to catch the school bus.

_____

4. The tired hikers <u>came</u> home.

_____

5. When the dog barked, the cat <u>went</u> under the fence.

_____

6. The chef loves to <u>make</u> fancy desserts.

_____

7. After the race, Billy <u>sat</u> on a blanket in the shade.

_____

8. "Where did I <u>put</u> my keys?" wondered Dad.

_____

Name ....

FIND THE ADJECTIVE

Mark the letter of the word that is an adjective.

1. Our <u>sun</u> <u>is</u> really a <u>special</u> <u>star</u>.
Ⓐ Ⓑ   Ⓒ   Ⓓ

2. <u>It</u> is a huge, <u>fiery</u> <u>ball</u> <u>in</u> the universe.
Ⓐ   Ⓑ   Ⓒ Ⓓ

3. The <u>sun</u> is <u>so</u> <u>hot</u> that it <u>can</u> heat the earth.
Ⓐ   Ⓑ Ⓒ   Ⓓ

4. The <u>bright</u> sun is hotter <u>than</u> all the <u>fires</u> on <u>earth</u>.
Ⓐ   Ⓑ   Ⓒ   Ⓓ

5. <u>Too</u> much sun can <u>burn</u> your <u>skin</u> and make you <u>sick</u>.
Ⓐ   Ⓑ   Ⓒ   Ⓓ

6. The <u>moon</u> is <u>our</u> <u>nearest</u> <u>neighbor</u> in space.
Ⓐ   Ⓑ   Ⓒ   Ⓓ

7. <u>Brave</u> <u>men</u> walked <u>on</u> the moon for the first <u>time</u> in 1969.
Ⓐ   Ⓑ   Ⓒ   Ⓓ

8. <u>During</u> the <u>month</u>, we can see the moon in <u>different</u> <u>shapes</u>.
Ⓐ   Ⓑ   Ⓒ   Ⓓ

9. The moon's <u>dark</u> spots are <u>called</u> *seas*, <u>but</u> <u>they</u> have
Ⓐ   Ⓑ   Ⓒ Ⓓ

no water.

10. Moon <u>soil</u> is <u>much</u> too <u>dry</u> for plants to <u>grow</u> there.
Ⓐ   Ⓑ   Ⓒ   Ⓓ

11. The <u>astronauts</u> <u>left</u> <u>jagged</u> <u>footprints</u> on the moon.
Ⓐ   Ⓑ   Ⓒ   Ⓓ

12. <u>Maybe</u> someday, <u>curious</u> <u>visitors</u> can <u>travel</u> to see them!
Ⓐ   Ⓑ   Ⓒ   Ⓓ

MAKE COMPARISONS

The word in **boldface** is an adjective. Write a different form of the adjective to complete each sentence. The first has been done for you.

1. Diego can run **fast**, but Carl is even _____faster_____.

2. Shelly is **older** than Rose, but Patty is the _____.

3. A cow is a **big** animal, but a moose is _____.

4. Plain pizza is **good**, but pizza with pepperoni is _____.

5. A **bad** cut can get _____ if you don't clean it well.

6. It will be a **funnier** joke if you use your _____ voice.

7. If one donut makes you **happy**, will two donuts make you _____?

8. Mom was **busy** before, but with the new baby she is _____ than ever.

9. The storm is **worse** now, but the _____ is yet to come.

10. Her eyes are _____ than the **bluest** ocean.

Name ....

USE A BETTER ADJECTIVE

These sentences have boring adjectives.
Rewrite each sentence, using a more exciting adjective.

1. That puppy has <u>nice</u> fur.

_____

2. The sunset was <u>pretty</u> tonight!

_____

3. The teacher's baby is <u>cute</u>.

_____

4. He read a <u>dumb</u> story.

_____

5. We ate at a <u>good</u> restaurant.

_____

6. New York is a really <u>great</u> city.

_____

7. She had a <u>fine</u> time at the party.

_____

Name ....

ANSWER WITH ADVERBS

Adverbs can tell *when*, *where*, *how*, or *how much*.
Answer each question using an adverb from the box below.
Make sure to write a full sentence.

always	**hungrily**	**loudly**	**never**
quickly	**sometimes**	**usually**	**very**

1. When do bears take a long sleep?

_____

_____

2. Where do bears do this sleeping?

_____

_____

3. How do bears eat when they finally wake up?

_____

_____

4. How does an angry bear's growl sound?

_____

_____

5. Where can you see a real bear?

_____

_____

Name ....

COMBINE TWO SENTENCES

Read each pair of short sentences. Write both ideas in one longer sentence. Use words from the box below to help you.

and	**because**	**but**	**for**
neither	**since**	**though**	

1. Dogs eat meat. Cows eat grain.

_____

_____

2. Greg plays hockey. Greg is on the hockey team.

_____

_____

3. Labor Day is in September. Flag Day is in June.

_____

_____

4. I picked a blue coat. My favorite color is blue.

_____

_____

5. Dinah likes to spell hard words. *Elephant* is a hard word.

_____

_____

USE FIGURES OF SPEECH

Circle the words that have the same meaning as the expression in **boldface**.

1. Hank is **all thumbs** today.
   a. clumsy
   b. sick
   c. sneaky
   d. happy

2. I'll **break the news** to her.
   a. help
   b. ignore
   c. tell
   d. hurt

3. Leah **eats like a bird**.
   a. gobbles her food
   b. picks at her food
   c. buries her food
   d. sings while she eats

4. They **got wind** of the plan.
   a. called off
   b. invented
   c. were mad about
   d. heard about

5. Won't you **have a heart**?
   a. fall in love
   b. be kind
   c. see the doctor
   d. take a nap

6. It's time to **hit the road** now.
   a. leave
   b. drive
   c. eat
   d. study

7. I can finally **let my hair down**.
   a. shower
   b. dress up
   c. relax
   d. dance

8. You'll just have to **sit tight**.
   a. snuggle down
   b. squeeze together
   c. be patient
   d. escape

EXPLAIN FIGURES OF SPEECH

Each sentence below has a figure of speech shown in **boldface**. Think about what those words mean. Rewrite each sentence. Keep the same meaning, but don't use the figure of speech.

1. As the teacher told the story, the class was **all ears**.

_____

_____

2. Don't **beat around the bush**—just say it!

_____

_____

3. One day, you will **eat your words**.

_____

_____

4. It's midnight! Shouldn't we **hit the hay**?

_____

_____

5. Those two never **see eye to eye** on anything.

_____

_____

SPELLING SOUNDS

In each row, draw an X in the boxes beside the two pictures whose word names begin with the same letters.

1. ☐	☐	☐
2. ☐	☐	☐
3. ☐	☐	☐
4. ☐	☐	☐
5. ☐	☐	☐
6. ☐	☐	☐

WRITE A WORD (1)

1. Write a word that starts with **pr**. _____

2. Write a word that starts with **fl**. _____

3. Write a word that starts with **dr**. _____

4. Write a word that starts with **sm**. _____

5. Write a word that starts with **sh** _____

6. Write a word that starts with **th**. _____

7. Write a word that starts with **kn**. _____

8. Write a word that starts with **qu**. _____

Name ....

WRITE A WORD (2)

1. Write a word that ends with **ft**. _____

2. Write a word that ends with **ld**. _____

3. Write a word that ends with **mp**. _____

4. Write a word that ends with **nch**. _____

5. Write a word that ends with **ng**. _____

6. Write a word that ends with **ck**. _____

7. Write a word that ends with **st**. _____

8. Write a word that ends with **sh**. _____

Name ....

SPELL CHECK

In each row, circle the word that is spelled wrong.
If all the words are spelled right, circle *No Mistake.*

1.	middle	midle	riddle	*No Mistake*
2.	large	garage	barje	*No Mistake*
3.	dancing	fencing	forced	*No Mistake*
4.	vacation	action	fraktion	*No Mistake*
5.	sleeve	believe	receive	*No Mistake*
6.	explane	unchain	against	*No Mistake*
7.	breakfast	lunch	dinnor	*No Mistake*
8.	square	skirt	scarf	*No Mistake*
9.	trinket	blankit	thankful	No *Mistake*
10.	measure	pleasant	lether	*No Mistake*
11.	childrun	different	problem	*No Mistake*
12.	meself	ourselves	selfish	*No Mistake*
13.	sugar	ashes	finish	*No Mistake*
14.	gentle	jungle	gardin	*No Mistake*
15.	turkey	monky	skunk	*No Mistake*

Name ....

SPELLING MISTAKES

Read each sentence. Decide which underlined word is spelled wrong. Fill in the circle beneath the misspelled word.

1. You <u>could</u> have <u>been</u> <u>hirt</u>.
Ⓐ Ⓑ Ⓒ

2. He <u>spild</u> the <u>milk</u> on the <u>kitchen</u> floor.
Ⓐ Ⓑ Ⓒ

3. <u>Who</u> did you work with at <u>sckool</u> <u>today</u>?
Ⓐ Ⓑ Ⓒ

4. Maybe we <u>kin</u> have <u>chicken</u> for <u>dinner</u>.
Ⓐ Ⓑ Ⓒ

5. They went to a <u>sunny</u> <u>iland</u> near the <u>ocean</u>.
Ⓐ Ⓑ Ⓒ

6. Mom works on the top <u>floor</u> of that <u>modern</u> <u>bilding</u>.
Ⓐ Ⓑ Ⓒ

7. <u>Everyware</u> we looked, <u>people</u> were holding <u>signs</u>.
Ⓐ Ⓑ Ⓒ

8. She ran to <u>anser</u> the phone <u>before</u> the ringing <u>stopped</u>.
Ⓐ Ⓑ Ⓒ

9. Cats who've had <u>enuff</u> to eat may <u>leave</u> food in the <u>bowl</u>.
Ⓐ Ⓑ Ⓒ

10. That <u>teacher</u> <u>aksed</u> us some hard <u>questions</u>.
Ⓐ Ⓑ Ⓒ

UPPERCASE AND LOWERCASE

Write the missing letters. Use a capital letter where it is needed.
Use a lowercase letter where it is needed.

1. H or **h**

_____is name is Spanish, but _____is parents are Chinese!

2. D or **d**

We _____id many fun things when we were in _____enver.

3. R or **r**

I live on Maple _____oad, _____ight near the library.

4. L or **l**

The _____ight was so low, _____inda couldn't read her book.

5. W or **w**

I _____onder where _____endy will have her party.

6. T or **t**

I _____ake vitamins every day, but on _____uesday I forgot.

7. I or **i**

My favorite food _____s pizza, but _____ also love shrimp.

8. S or **s**

The knight, _____ir John, was a _____trong warrior.

FORM COMPOUND WORDS

A compound word is made of two shorter words.
Snowflake is a compound word made from *snow + flake*.

Match a word in List A with another word in List B
to make four compound words.
Write your compound words on lines 1 through 4.

LIST A	LIST B
jelly	day
base	fish
back	ball
birth	pack

I. _____

2. _____

3. _____

4. _____

Now write a sentence for each compound word you formed.

5. _____

_____

6. _____

_____

7. _____

_____

8. _____

_____

HOMOPHONES

Be careful! Some words sound alike but have different spellings. Pick the correct word for each sentence. Write it on the line.

ate or **eight**	**1.** Our car is _____ years old.
hole or **whole**	**2.** He learned the _____ poem by heart.
meat or **meet**	**3.** May we _____ the queen?
plain or **plane**	**4.** She wore a _____ white dress.
blew or **blue**	**5.** Winds _____ the leaves off the trees.
right or **write**	**6.** It's time to _____ that note.
flour or **flower**	**7.** The cake needs two cups of _____.
one or **won**	**8.** Did you hear who _____ the race?
pair or **pear**	**9.** Tom knit a _____ of red socks.
weak or **week**	**10.** They will be away for one _____.

END MARKS

Write the best end mark. Use ■ **or** ? **or** !.

1. Who is your teacher ___

2. Oh no, my team lost ___

3. Let's meet after school ___

4. Can we get a dog ___

5. Stop right now ___

6. Why is the water running ___

7. It is cool today ___

8. Hey, leave my toys alone ___

9. What is Mom's favorite color ___

10. That was a big problem ___

WATCH THE PUNCTUATION

Shade the box beside the sentence that has NO punctuation mistake.

1. [A] They wont eat those snacks.
  [B] We can't have any more.
  [C] Mrs. Hardy doesnt' know how to swim.

2. [A] He was born on September 30 1996.
  [B] Dad cannot find his gray sock's.
  [C] Let's have some ice cream.

3. [A] Chicago is called "The Windy City."
  [B] St Paul is the capital, of Minnesota.
  [C] Texas, is the Lone Star State.

4. [A] Do you want? to play checkers
  [B] Are you almost done.
  [C] Those speed skaters go so fast!

5. [A] The dessert was warm, gooey, and delicious.
  [B] Our flag is red white, and blue.
  [C] The cats are named, Socks Tiger and Puffy.

6. [A] School ends at 300 P.M.
  [B] We have dinner at 6:00 P.M.
  [C] We go to bed at 9;30 P.M.

7. [A] Mount. Sunflower is the highest point in Kansas.
  [B] E. B White wrote *Stuart Little*.
  [C] This is Dr. Mary Diamond, my dentist.

PART 3:

STEPS OF THE WRITING PROCESS

PREWRITING: DRAW A PICTURE

What will you see at an amusement park?
Draw pictures.
List words and ideas, too.

_____

_____

_____

_____

_____

_____

_____

_____

_____

_____

_____

PREWRITING: MAKE AN IDEA WEB

Pretend that your class is studying spiders.
Fill in the web with ideas to learn about spiders.

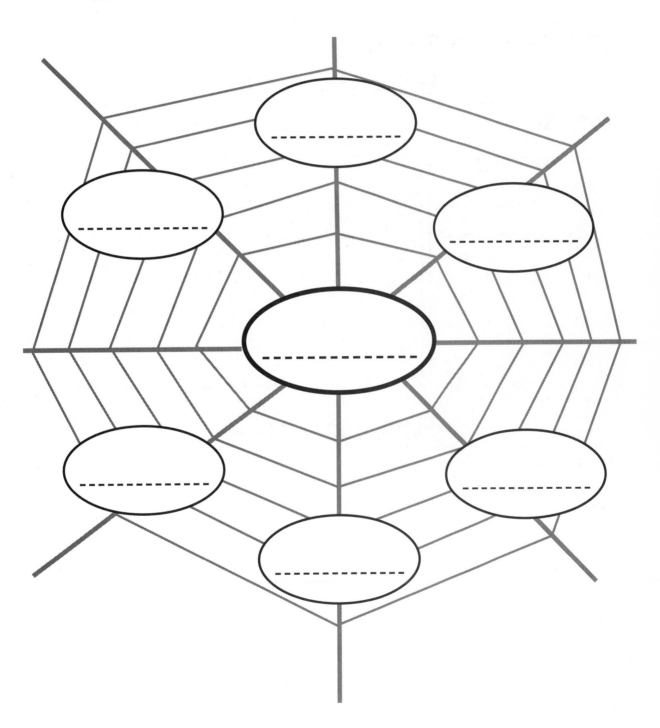

PREWRITING: BUILD STORY BLOCKS

Plan a story for each title below. Then fill in the blocks with your ideas for that title. Tell where the story takes place. Then write what happens in the beginning, middle, and end. List ideas to make the story fun to read.

Lost on an Island!

Setting:		
Beginning	**Middle**	**End**

Who Has a Key?

Setting:		
Beginning	**Middle**	**End**

Name ....

PREWRITING: USE A CHARACTER MAP

Make up a character for a story.
Use this map to plan what this character is like.

LOOKS

_____
_____
_____
_____
_____

PERSONALITY

_____
_____
_____
_____
_____

The Character's Name:

_____

FEELINGS

_____
_____
_____
_____
_____

HABITS

_____
_____
_____
_____
_____

Name ....

PREWRITING: WHAT DO YOU SEE?

Look at the picture of the computer lab.
Take notes about what you see. List lots of good details.

_____

_____

_____

_____

_____

_____

_____

PREWRITING: I KNOW, I WANT TO KNOW

Look at each picture. Write something you know about it.
Write something you want to know about it.

PICTURE	I KNOW...	I WANT TO KNOW...
1.		
2.		
3.		
4.		
5.		

PREWRITING: ASK QUESTIONS (1)

Imagine an airplane pilot visits your class.
What questions would you ask? Write them below.

1. What _____

_____ **?**

2. Who _____

_____ **?**

3. How _____

_____ **?**

4. When _____

_____ **?**

5. Why _____

_____ **?**

6. Where _____

_____ **?**

Name ....

PREWRITING: ASK QUESTIONS (2)

Pretend you are a reporter.
Write two questions to ask **each person.**

This is Marvin the Mighty.
He is a famous strong man.
What do you want to ask him?

1. _____

_____

_____

2. _____

_____

_____

This is Sally Kent.
She trains horses.
What do you want to ask her?

1. _____

_____

_____

2. _____

_____

_____

Name ....

PREWRITING: ASK QUESTIONS (3)

Pretend you are a reporter.
Write two questions to ask each person.

This is Dr. Lisa.
She is a scientist. She studies mice.
What do you want to ask her?

1. _____

_____

_____

2. _____

_____

_____

This is Gary.
He is a basketball player.
What do you want to ask him?

1. _____

_____

_____

2. _____

_____

_____

Name ....

DRAFTING: WHICH BELONGS?

Mark the correct box.

1. Which belongs in a car?

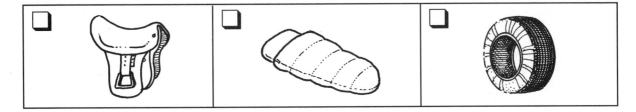

2. Which belongs at the library?

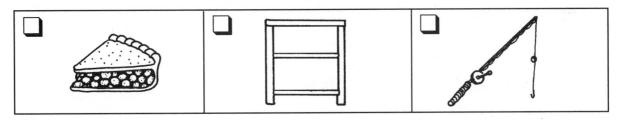

3. Which belongs in the freezer?

Now choose one: a car, the library, or the freezer. Write a good topic sentence for the start of a story about it.

_____

_____

_____

_____

DRAFTING: SUPPORTING DETAILS

Read each topic sentence.
Then write two more sentences that add supporting details.

1. It was a quiet day at the pet shop.

_____

_____

_____

_____

2. The teacher was looking all through her desk for something.

_____

_____

_____

_____

3. At the top of the Ferris wheel we stopped moving.

_____

_____

_____

_____

Name ....

DRAFTING: BEGINNING, MIDDLE, END

Pick a topic from the box below. Write a short story about it.
Be sure your little story has a beginning, a middle, and an end.
Don't forget to write the title.

What a Party!	Learning to Skate	I Can't Fall Asleep

Title: _____

Beginning: _____

_____

_____

_____

Middle: _____

_____

_____

_____

End: _____

_____

_____

_____

DRAFTING: ORGANIZE A STORY

Write the sentences in an order that tells a story.
Add details to make the story complete.

1. He was in a happy mood.
Dad took us to a restaurant.
Dad came home early.
"I have some good news," he said.

_____

_____

_____

_____

2. What a mess!
It stuck to the pan.
We made oatmeal.
We spilled the milk.

_____

_____

_____

_____

Name ....

DRAFTING: WRITE THE STEPS

Tell how to play tic-tac-toe. Write the steps in order.
Give the important information. Use as many steps as you need.

1. _____

   _____

   _____

   _____

2. _____

   _____

   _____

3. _____

   _____

   _____

4. _____

   _____

   _____

5. _____

   _____

   _____

6. _____

   _____

   _____

Name ....

DRAFTING: LEAVE A MESSAGE

Mrs. Lopez calls. She wants to talk to Mom. But Mom is out. Leave Mom a note. Tell her about the call.

DRAFTING: WRITE A REVIEW

Think of a movie you saw, a book you read, or a TV show you watched. Write about it. Tell what you liked, what you did not like, and why. Tell whether others would like it.

_____

_____

_____

_____

_____

_____

_____

_____

_____

_____

_____

DRAFTING: DESCRIBE A DREAM

Think about a dream you had. It can be a good dream, a bad dream, or an odd dream. Write about it. Use lots of describing words. Make the reader want to keep reading!

_____

_____

_____

_____

_____

_____

_____

_____

_____

_____

_____

_____

DRAFTING: SORT THE SENTENCES

Read the four topics in the box below. Then read the sentences that follow. Write A, B, C, or D to match each sentence with the correct topic.

> **A.** Training a New Pet
> **B.** How to Build a Fire
> **C.** At the Hospital
> **D.** My First Plane Ride

_____ **1.** The visiting hours were printed on the door.

_____ **2.** I felt so lucky that the window seat was mine!

_____ **3.** Wet wood will make too much smoke.

_____ **4.** Be firm, but gentle, and don't use too many words.

_____ **5.** It is not easy to teach a pet how to behave.

_____ **6.** Set the wood in a fireplace or inside a ring of stones.

_____ **7.** Always ask if the patient may have visitors.

_____ **8.** We got to the airport two hours early.

_____ **9.** Keep a pail of water nearby, just in case.

_____ **10.** The flight crew was very friendly to me.

_____ **11.** If the patient is getting tired, it's time to leave.

_____ **12.** A well-trained pet makes a better family member.

EDITING: MAKE IT BETTER

Read each plain sentence. Think about how to make it more lively and more fun to read. Then rewrite the sentence.

1. There were clouds in the sky.

_____

_____

2. The horse walked along the trail.

_____

_____

3. They watched from behind the bushes.

_____

_____

4. The doorbell rang loudly.

_____

_____

5. Where did we leave that map?

_____

_____

EDITING: REMOVE EXTRA DETAILS

Each paragraph below has a sentence that doesn't belong. Find that sentence and cross it out.

1. The lamp won't go on. We check the cord, but it is plugged in. We check the bulb, but it works in another lamp. The television works fine. Maybe the lamp switch is broken.

2. The new kittens are so tiny! Their eyes are not open yet. Three of them are gray and two are white. The mama cat likes squeaky toys. We'll give away the kittens when they get older.

3. The line at the theater was very long. The tickets cost $7 for adults and $4 for kids. We waited for more than a half hour to see the new adventure film. After all, it was opening day.

4. I want to take harp lessons. Amy works at a music store. She knows a lot about guitars and drums. She answers people's questions. She works the cash register and answers the phone.

EDITING: PICK THE SENTENCE

Read each group of words. Find the group that is a complete sentence. Shade the letter beside that group.

1.
- A Playing in the sand.
- B At the park.
- C Near the top of the hill.
- D Let's dig in the sand.

2.
- A Loud and clear.
- B So we can hear.
- C Turn up the radio.
- D Picked that station.

3.
- A Grapes and bananas.
- B He made a fruit salad.
- C In the big bowl.
- D On the kitchen counter.

4.
- A The first library.
- B Had very few books.
- C It was in an old house.
- D Only one librarian.

5.
- A May I have some tea?
- B Too hot to drink now.
- C Without sugar?
- D In a cup and saucer.

6.
- A Using finger paint.
- B Made a poster.
- C For the science project.
- D They worked together.

7.
- A It was my first time.
- B Learning to dive.
- C Climbed the ladder.
- D Afraid to jump at first.

8.
- A Directions to the party.
- B Here is the map.
- C Having a great time!
- D Lots of guests.

9.
- A Bears and lions.
- B Roaming free.
- C The new zoo is open.
- D Safe for the animals.

10.
- A With your parents?
- B Will you please call later?
- C After the movie is over.
- D With my birthday money.

EDITING: CHOOSE THE BEST SENTENCE

Choose the sentence in each group that sounds the best.

1. A The sun looks like an orange ball.
B Like an orange ball looks the sun.
C An orange ball the sun looks like.

2. A Outside my window a nest built by birds.
B Birds outside my window built a nest.
C Birds built a nest outside my window.

3. A Dan goes to bed earlier always than do I.
B Dan always goes to bed earlier than I do.
C Dan goes always to bed earlier I do than.

4. A Do you like that new book?
B That new book, do you like?
C Do you that new book like?

5. A The ranger of the cave took us on a tour.
B Of the cave the ranger on a tour took us.
C The ranger took us on a tour of the cave.

6. A I like of my cat to draw pictures.
B I like to draw pictures of my cat.
C My cat to draw pictures I like.

7. A Pancakes that looked like stars made Dad.
B Dad made stars that looked like pancakes.
C Dad made pancakes that looked like stars.

8. A Sometimes we have eggs for supper.
B We have sometimes eggs for supper.
C Sometimes for supper have we eggs.

EDITING: FIX THE MISTAKES

Here is the first draft of a letter. It has some mistakes.
Each mistake is underlined. Find the answer choices that go
with each underlined error. Choose the best answer to fix
the mistake.

① March 26 2002

② Dear Mrs Kelly?
③ Id like some information. My class is
learning about boats. We hear that your
museum ④ in Camden maine has many
model boats to see. Is this true? Can our
class visit? When are you open?
⑤ please answer Soon. We hope to visit
⑥ in april! Thanks for your help.

Your friend,

Chip A. Hoy

I. A march 26, 2002
B March 26: 2002
C March 26, 2002

2. A Dear Mrs. Kelly?
B Dear Mrs. Kelly,
C Dear Mrs. Kelly.

3. A I'd like
B I had like
C I will like

4. A in Camden, maine,
B in Camden, Maine,
C in camden, maine,

5. A Please answer Soon.
B Please Answer Soon.
C Please answer soon.

6. A in april.
B in April.
C in April?

PART 4:

RESEARCHING AND GATHERING INFORMATION

LIBRARY RESOURCES (1)

Read the information in the box below.
Then answer the questions about library materials.

> **Ben is getting a new fish tank. He wants to find a library book that can give him some useful information.**

1. In which area of the library will Ben find a book that will help him?

  A fiction
  B biography
  C nonfiction
  D sports

2. Which book would tell Ben about caring for fish?

  A an atlas
  B a book on pets
  C an art book
  D a dictionary

3. Ben knows the name of a book to get. What part of the card catalog should he check?

  A subject card
  B index card
  C author card
  D title card

4. Ben found the book. Where in it will Ben find the name of the author?

  A in the glossary
  B in the index
  C on the title page
  D in the table of contents

5. Ben wonders if the book tells about saltwater fish. He could check

  A in Chapter 5.
  B in the index.
  C on the book jacket.
  D in a review.

6. Ben wonders what year this book was published. This fact is called

  A the spine.
  B the dedication.
  C the call number.
  D the copyright date.

LIBRARY RESOURCES (2)

Mark the best answer to each question below.

1. Nancy wants to know about Dr. Martin Luther King, Jr. In which volume of the encyclopedia will she look?

- [A] D
- [B] M
- [C] L
- [D] K

2. Paul is writing a report on submarines. Which book might help him?

- [A] *Ships of Ancient Egypt*
- [B] *Modern Ocean Vessels*
- [C] *Into Outer Space*
- [D] *Sea World, USA*

3. Libby wants to see a map of Mexico. Which is the best source for her to check?

- [A] an atlas
- [B] a dictionary
- [C] a cookbook
- [D] a Spanish magazine

4. Eli is looking up the word *waif*. To which part of the dictionary should he turn?

- [A] the beginning
- [B] the middle
- [C] the end
- [D] cannot tell

5. Hallie wants to learn the meaning of *reckon*. It will be on the dictionary page that has which guide words?

- [A] reach / rebus
- [B] recall / record
- [C] red / reek
- [D] remember / repeat

6. Joe wants to see pictures of underground passages. Which might be the best place for him to look?

- [A] an adventure video
- [B] a science filmstrip
- [C] a CD-ROM on caves
- [D] Web site for New York

WRITE TOGETHER: GROUP STORIES

Write a group story with your students. Work through the steps of the writing process with a small group or with the whole class. Invite children to suggest sentences, descriptions, conclusions, questions, dialogue, illustrations, and so on. Record the story on chart paper, an overhead projector, or the chalkboard. Encourage children to help revise the story to make it better.

Here are some ideas for group stories:

- Write a story about something sad.

- Write a story about something odd.

- Write a story about something funny.

- Write a story about something old.

- Write a story about a shock.

- Write a story about a daydream.

- Write a story about a ghost.

- Write a story about an unusual trip.

BUBBLE PRACTICE SHEET

Write your name in the boxes below, then fill in the bubble for each letter.

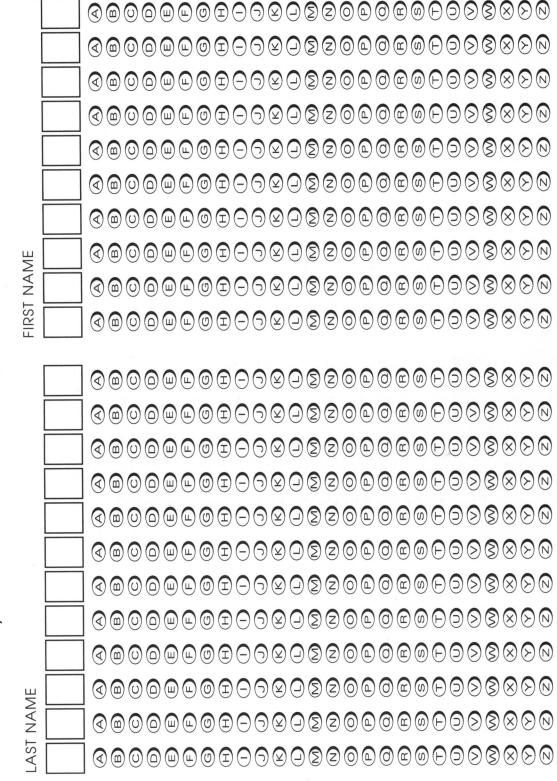

WRITER'S SELF-EVALUATION CHECKLIST

Use this checklist to check your writing.

- ❏ Does every sentence have a complete thought?
- ❏ Does every sentence start with a capital letter?
- ❏ Did I use the right end marks?
- ❏ Did I indent new paragraphs?
- ❏ Did I stick to my topic?
- ❏ Did I leave out any words?
- ❏ Did I give enough details and facts?
- ❏ Does my piece say what I want it to say?
- ❏ Does my introduction grab readers?
- ❏ Does my piece have a clear ending?
- ❏ Did I check my grammar?
- ❏ Did I check my spelling?
- ❏ Is my handwriting neat and clear?
- ❏ Did I remember to write a title?

TEACHER NOTES and SELECTED ANSWERS

Test-Taking Practice; More Test-Taking Practice (pp. 7–8)

Provide additional practice with any type of directions children have difficulty with.

Part 1: General Concepts of Writing

Plan a Trip; Make a List; Invite a Friend; Leave a Note; Make a Chart; Finish the Chart (pp. 10–15)

Evaluate open-ended activities in terms of children's ability to communicate key ideas.

Labels (1) (p. 16)

1. gate   2. toe or big toe   3. eye or wink
4. pouch or baby   5. arm   6. fire or flame

Labels (2) (p. 17)

1. bun or roll or hot dog   2. cloud or rain or storm   3. gas or pump   4. wing   5. logs or fire   6. stamp

Write a Word (p. 18)

Sample answers: 1. chin   2. shoe   3. prize
4. sneeze   5. trick   6. clown   7. thing
8. spark   9. white   10. drink

Words and Spaces; Tell About It (1, 2) (pp. 19–21)

Evaluate in terms of children's ability to communicate key ideas.

Make a Sentence (p. 22)

1. The cat is old.   2. Where are my slippers?
3. Let's bake some cookies.   4. This book is too hard.   5. Who knows the right answer?

Write Some More (p. 23)

Evaluate children's ability to complete a sentence and write a second sentence that continues the idea.

Name the Group (1) (p. 24)

1. feathers   2. cameras   3. boats.
Sentences will vary.

Name the Group (2) (p. 25)

1. kitchen tools   2. shapes   3. shells.
Sentences will vary.

Finish the Paragraphs (p. 26)

Evaluate children's ability to stick to the main idea of the given paragraph.

Put in Order (1) (p. 27)

Order: 1, 3, 2; stories will vary.

Put in Order (2) (p. 28)

Order: 3, 4, 2, 1; stories will vary.

What Happened Before?; What Happens Next?; Tell a Story (1, 2); Write a Report; Take a Message (pp. 29–34)

Evaluate children's explanation, story, and clarity of details.

Part 2: Conventions of Grammar, Mechanics, and Style

Find the Noun (p. 36)

1. C   2. B   3. D   4. B   5. C   6. A   7. D
8. C   9. D   10. D   11. D   12. A

Noun Names (p. 37)

1. thing   2. place   3. persons   4. thing or idea   5. person   6. persons   7. thing
8. idea.   9. things   10. idea   11. person
12. idea

Write the Plural (p. 38)

2. soldiers   3. desks   4. benches
5. foxes   6. cities   7. families   8. turkeys
9. leaves   10. lives   11. children   12. men
13. feet   14. geese   15. deer

Write the Singular (p. 39)

2. apple   3. chair   4. lunch   5. box
6. candy   7. berry   8. monkey   9. knife
10. half   11. hero   12. echo   13. sheep
14. woman   15. mouse

Pick the Pronoun (p. 40)

1. c   2. a   3. d   4. a   5. c   6. b   7. b   8. c
9. d   10. a

Find the Verb (p. 41)

1. C   2. B   3. C   4. C   5. A   6. B   7. A   8. C
9. B   10. B   11. C   12. A

Pick the Verb Form (p. 42)

1. a   2. b   3. b   4. a   5. b   6. b   7. a   8. c
9. b   10. c

Use the Verb (p. 43)

Evaluate sentences on completion, clarity, and correct usage of the given verb.

Use Verb Tenses (p. 44)

2. blow   3. drank   4. dug
5. brought   6. forget   7. leave   8. seen
9. told   10. wrote

Use a Better Verb (p. 45)

Answers will vary. Sample answers: 1. strutted,

TEACHER NOTES and SELECTED ANSWERS

raced, sauntered   2. gobbled, chomped, gulped   3. raced, flew, sprinted   4. plodded, trudged, limped   5. dove, crept, scurried   6. create, whip up, invent   7. sprawled, plopped, relaxed   8. deposit, leave, throw

Find the Adjective (p. 46)
2. B   3. C   4. A   5. D   6. C   7. A   8. C   9. A   10. C   11. C   12. B

Make Comparisons (p. 47)
2. oldest   3. bigger   4. better   5. worse   6. funny/funniest   7. happier   8. busier   9. worst   10. bluer

Use a Better Adjective (p. 48)
Answers will vary. Sample answers: 1. silky, thick, lush   2. colorful, glorious, spectacular   3. adorable, chubby, darling   4. foolish, ridiculous, pointless   5. luxurious, fancy, stylish   6. magnificent, breathtaking, amazing   7. enjoyable, pleasing, entertaining

Answer With Adverbs (p. 49)
Sentences will vary. Sample answers: 1. Bears always take a long sleep in the winter.   2. Bears usually sleep in a cave.   3. They eat hungrily.   4. The growl of an angry bear rings loudly through the air.   5. You can sometimes see a real bear in a zoo.

Combine Two Sentences (p. 50)
Combined sentences may vary. Sample answers: 1. but   2. since, because   3. but   4. because, for, since   5. and

Use Figures of Speech (p. 51)
1. a   2. c   3. b   4. d   5. b   6. a   7. c   8. c

Explain Figures of Speech (p. 52)
Revisions will vary. Sample answers: 1. As the teacher told the story, the class listened closely.   2. Don't stall, just say it.   3. One day, you'll wish you hadn't said that.   4. It's midnight! Shouldn't we go to sleep?   5. Those two never agree on anything.

Spelling Sounds (p. 53)
1. phone/photographs   2. queen/question mark   3. shovel/shark   4. thimble/thirty   5. knife/knot   6. skunk/skateboard

Write a Word (1, 2) (pp. 54-55)
Answers will vary. Check that students

have written words that begin (or end) with the given sound(s).

Spell Check (p. 56)
1. midle   2. barje   3. No Mistake   4. fraktion   5. No Mistake   6. explane   7. dinnor   8. No Mistake   9. blankit   10. lether   11. childrun   12. meself   13. No Mistake   14. gardin   15. monky

Spelling Mistakes (p. 57)
1. C   2. A   3. B   4. A   5. B   6. C   7. A   8. A   9. A   10. B

Uppercase and Lowercase (p. 58)
1. H/h   2. d/D   3. R/r   4. l/L   5. w/W   6. t/T   7. i/I   8. S/s

Form Compound Words (p. 59)
1-4. jellyfish, baseball, backpack, birthday   5-8. Evaluate sentences on clarity and completeness.

Homophones (p. 60)
1. eight   2. whole   3. meet   4. plain   5. blew   6. write   7. flour   8. won   9. pair   10. week

End Marks (p. 61)
1. ?   2. !   3. .   4. ?   5. !   6. ?   7. .   8. !   9. ?   10. !

Watch the Punctuation (p. 62)
1. B   2. C   3. A   4. C   5. A   6. B   7. C

Part 3: Steps of the Writing Process

Prewriting activities (pp. 64-72)
Evaluate each activity in terms of completeness, clarity, cohesion, and children's ability to communicate responses that satisfy the given task.

Drafting: Which Belongs? (p. 73)
1. spare tire   2. bookshelf   3. ice-cube tray. Topic sentences will vary.

Drafting: Supporting Details (p. 74)
Supporting sentences will vary. Evaluate whether they follow the topic sentence.

Drafting: Beginning, Middle, End (p. 75)
Stories will vary. Evaluate for order, clarity, and completeness.

Drafting: Organize a Story (p. 76)
Sample responses: 1. Dad came home early

TEACHER NOTES and SELECTED ANSWERS

Monday. He was in a very happy mood. "I have some good news," he said. Dad took us all to a restaurant. There he shared his news.   2. We made oatmeal by ourselves. It stuck to the pan. We spilled the milk on the floor. What a mess we made!

Drafting: Write the Steps (p. 77)

Steps will vary. Evaluate for order, completeness, clarity, and the inclusion of key information.

Drafting activities (pp. 78–80)

Drafts will vary; evaluate for clarity, completeness, and how well the children communicated their ideas on the topic.

Drafting: Sort the Sentences (p. 81)

1. C   2. D   3. B   4. A   5. A   6. B   7. C
8. D   9. B   10. D   11. C   12. A

Editing: Make It Better (p. 82)

Revisions will vary. Sample answers:
1. There were fluffy white clouds in the blue sky.   2. The chestnut horse walked slowly but surely along the rugged trail.
3. They watched silently from behind the thick berry bushes.   4. The front doorbell rang loudly, interrupting our dinner.
5. Where did we leave that road map of how to get to the lake?

Editing: Remove Extra Details (p. 83)

1. The television works fine.   2. The mama cat likes squeaky toys.   3. The tickets cost $7 for adults and $4 for kids.   4. I want to take harp lessons.

Editing: Pick the Sentence (p. 84)

1. D   2. C   3. B   4. C   5. A   6. D   7. A
8. B   9. C   10. B

Editing: Choose the Best Sentence (p. 85)

1. A   2. C   3. B   4. A   5. C   6. B   7. C   8. A

Editing: Fix the Mistakes (p. 86)

1. C   2. B   3. A   4. B   5. C   6. B

Part 4: Researching and Gathering Information

Library Resources (1) (p. 88)

1. C   2. B   3. D   4. C   5. B   6. D

Library Resources (2) (p. 89)

1. D   2. B   3. A   4. C   5. B   6. C

NOTES